BEGINNING HISTORY

MEDIEVAL MARKETS

Barry Steel

Illustrated by Michael Bragg

BEGINNING HISTORY

Crusaders
Egyptian Pyramids
Greek Cities
Medieval Markets
Norman Castles
Roman Soldiers
Saxon Villages
Tudor Sailors
Victorian Children
Viking Explorers

All words that appear in **bold** are explained in the glossary on page 22.

Series Editor: Catherine Ellis
Book Editor: Dee Turner
Designer: Helen White

First published in 1989 by Wayland (Publishers) Limited, 61 Western Road, Hove, East Sussex BN3 1JD
© Copyright 1989 Wayland (Publishers) Ltd.

British Library Cataloguing in Publication Data
Steel, Barry
Medieval markets.
1. Markets, history
I. Title   II. Series
381′.18′09

ISBN 1–85210–814–2

Typeset by Kalligraphics Limited, Horley, Surrey.
Printed in Italy by G. Canale & C.S.p.A., Turin.
Bound in Belgium by Casterman, S.A.

CONTENTS

MEDIEVAL MARKETS

The earliest markets were small, like this one. Local people went there to sell or swap the things they had made or grown.

The **Middle Ages** lasted from about AD1000 to 1500. Most people in **medieval** times lived in country villages. Even those who lived in towns were close to fields, because nearly all towns were much smaller than they are today. Many people grew most of their food and made their own clothes. Some also made their own simple furniture, and even built their own houses.

Sometimes, however, people grew or made more than they needed for themselves. Markets began as places where they could take these goods and exchange them for things they could not make. Most of the things in the markets were simple, everyday goods such as food, cloth, shoes, pots, pans and knives. Almost everything was produced close to the market, and most customers lived nearby. They had to be near enough to walk to the market, do their trading, and walk home on the same day.

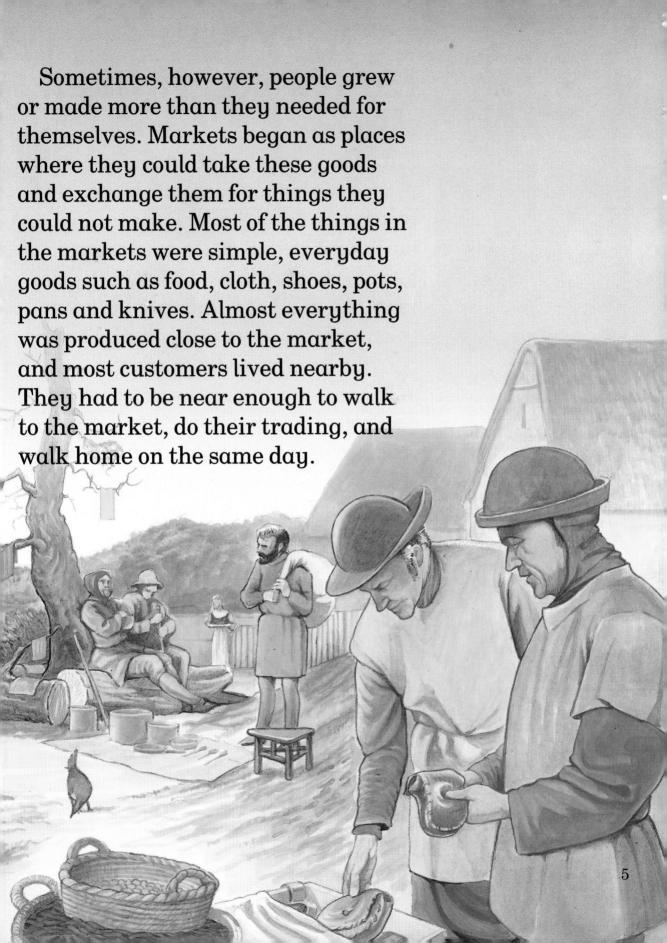

HOW MARKETS GREW

Many markets began at places where people could meet easily – like river bridges or crossroads. Potters, blacksmiths and other **craftsmen** found it best to build their workshops near the markets, and so villages and towns grew up. As villages and towns became larger, so did markets.

In some countries the ruler controlled the markets. The right to run markets was sold to important local people, who made money by charging the stallholders. Some markets were run by noble lords and

Above *The market cross in Salisbury, England.*

Below *People are selling geese and chickens at this stall.*

barons, others by churches and **monasteries**. Many markets were held after church on Sunday mornings, so that people who had to walk a long way to church could do their buying and selling at the same time. Sometimes, beautiful shelters, with a cross on top, were built for market traders. They are called market crosses. Some can still be seen in towns in Europe.

Markets often grew up near churches. Sometimes they were held on Sundays, after the church service.

7

MARKET FOLK

Above *Pedlars carried their goods from town to town.*

Below *A band of minstrels.*

When people came to market it was not just to buy and sell. They also enjoyed meeting friends and watching the noisy, colourful crowds. The air was filled with the cries of the stallholders selling fresh fruit and vegetables, butter, eggs and cheese, and with the delicious smells of their wares. Other sounds came from the workshops of craftsmen, such as the **blacksmith**, carpenter and potter, as they carried on working while waiting for their next customer.

The poorest people had no stalls. They simply spread their goods on the ground, or sold from baskets. There were also **pedlars** who travelled from place to place carrying their goods for sale. Among the crowds ran dogs and cats looking for scraps of food. Horses and donkeys plodded along loaded with goods, or pulling heavy wagons. Sometimes there were **minstrels**, acrobats, **jugglers**, performing animals and other entertainers.

A lively crowd at a market.

Money, Weights and Measures

The man on the right is weighing things in a balance scale. The other man is measuring cloth with a yardstick.

In a medieval market, people did not always use money for trading. It was quite normal to exchange or 'swap' things. For example, someone might exchange an animal for a piece of furniture. This was called **bartering**. But as time went on, buying and selling with money became more usual. The most common coin was the

silver penny. Prices were much lower than now – for example a pig might be sold for as little as 2 pennies (about 1p). Of course wages were also a lot less, perhaps only 10p or 15p a week.

Lengths were measured using inches (three grains of barley laid end to end), feet (the length of a man's foot), or yards (the distance between the end of a man's nose and the thumb of his outstretched arm). Liquids were measured in gallons (about 4·5 litres), quarts (about 1 litre) and pints (0·5 litre). Goods were weighed on a balance scale using pound weights (about 0·5 kilogram), ounces and grains.

CHEATING AND PUNISHMENTS

A cheat in the pillory. People are throwing rotten food at him.

There were always a few traders who tried to cheat their customers. They might use light weights on the balance scales, or their measuring jugs and **yardsticks** might be a little too small. Sometimes they put water in beer or wine, or added sawdust or stones to sacks of corn to make them weigh more.

In well-organized markets, men were paid to check on weights,

measures and scales, and to inspect goods for quality. There were special market courts where dishonest traders were tried. If they were found guilty they might expect to spend a day in the **stocks** or **pillory**. Then people would come and pelt them with rotten fruit, vegetables and other rubbish.

A fishmonger or butcher who gave poor value might be pulled through the market on a sledge, with a piece of stinking meat or fish hanging round his neck.

A man being punished in the stocks.

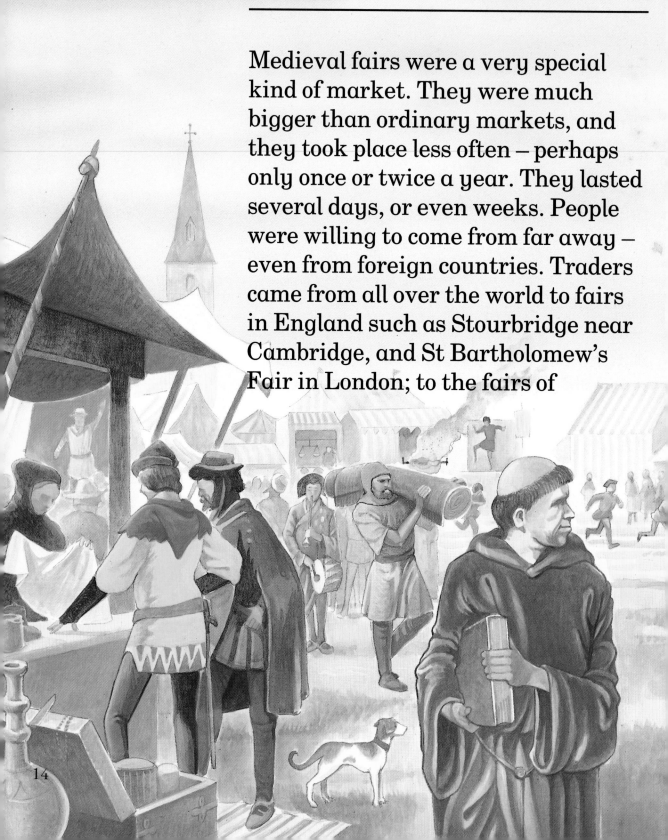

FAIRS

Medieval fairs were a very special kind of market. They were much bigger than ordinary markets, and they took place less often – perhaps only once or twice a year. They lasted several days, or even weeks. People were willing to come from far away – even from foreign countries. Traders came from all over the world to fairs in England such as Stourbridge near Cambridge, and St Bartholomew's Fair in London; to the fairs of

Champagne in France, and Nizhniy Novgorod in Russia. Many **merchants** spent their lives travelling huge distances on foot or horseback from one fair to the next. They brought luxury goods never seen at ordinary markets – precious metals and stones, silks, spices and perfumes from distant countries.

Organizing a fair was a difficult task. Town **councils** had to pay for the right to run a fair, so they charged **tolls** and rents to stallholders. Some fairs were organized by the Church.

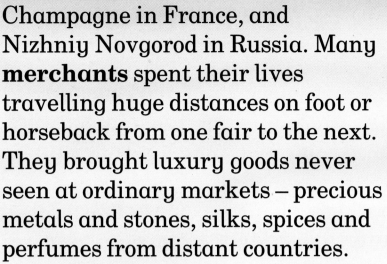

Fairs were large markets. Merchants and customers travelled long distances to buy and sell there.

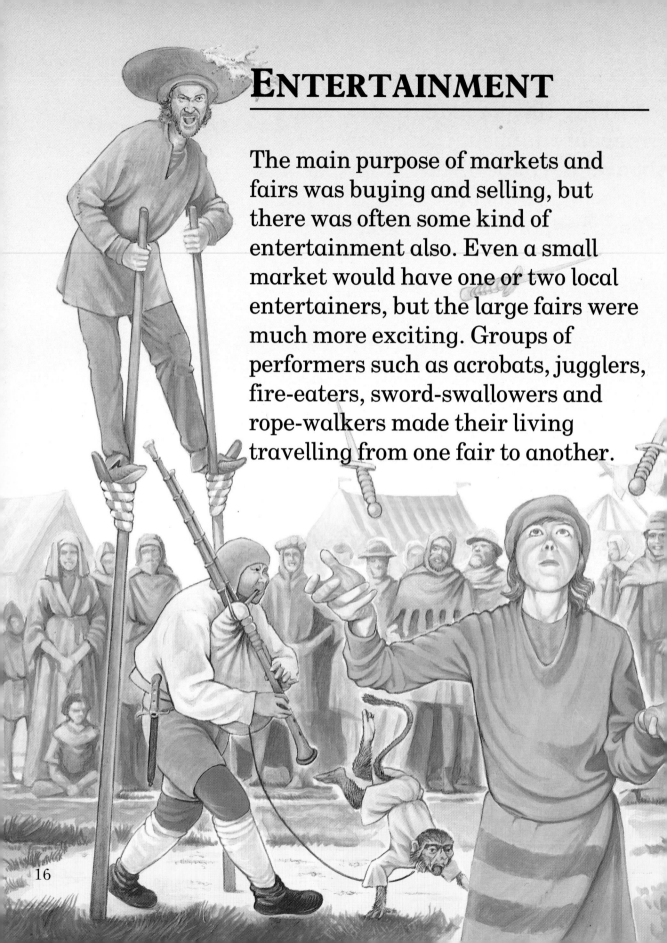

ENTERTAINMENT

The main purpose of markets and fairs was buying and selling, but there was often some kind of entertainment also. Even a small market would have one or two local entertainers, but the large fairs were much more exciting. Groups of performers such as acrobats, jugglers, fire-eaters, sword-swallowers and rope-walkers made their living travelling from one fair to another.

Left *Knights jousting. They are trying to knock each other off their horses.*

Sometimes there were strange performing animals from distant lands. The crowds particularly enjoyed the tricks of the dancing bears and monkeys. There were also sporting events such as **jousting** and wrestling. There might sometimes be a chance for people from the crowd to join in the fun and games.

In time the entertainment side of fairs became more important and the trading side grew less. Gradually fairs changed into the kind of fairground we know today, which is purely for fun, not for selling goods.

Below *This medieval picture shows people doing balancing tricks.*

LIVESTOCK AND FISH MARKETS

A market selling live animals and other goods.

People in towns could not keep enough animals for all the meat they needed, so special livestock markets developed. These were where live animals were bought and sold. It was not possible to kill animals on the farms and then take the meat to towns, because transport was very slow and there was no way to keep meat fresh for long periods. It was

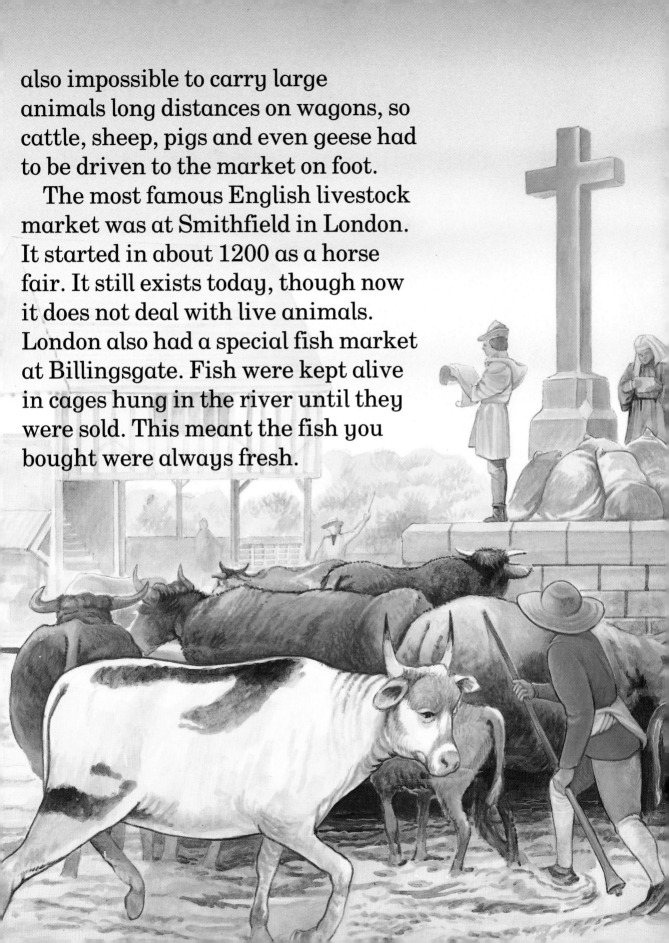

also impossible to carry large animals long distances on wagons, so cattle, sheep, pigs and even geese had to be driven to the market on foot.

The most famous English livestock market was at Smithfield in London. It started in about 1200 as a horse fair. It still exists today, though now it does not deal with live animals. London also had a special fish market at Billingsgate. Fish were kept alive in cages hung in the river until they were sold. This meant the fish you bought were always fresh.

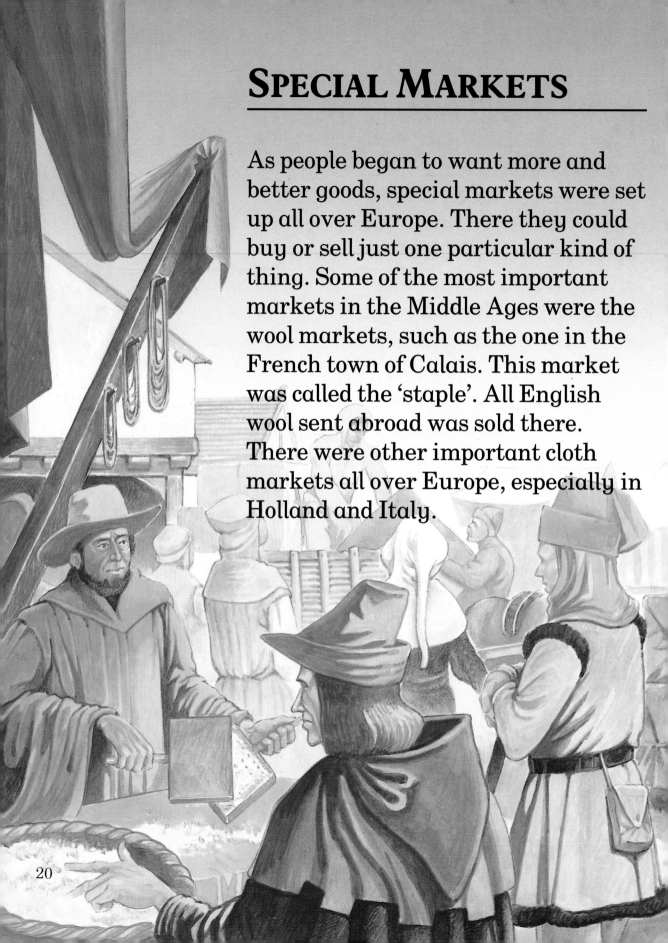

SPECIAL MARKETS

As people began to want more and better goods, special markets were set up all over Europe. There they could buy or sell just one particular kind of thing. Some of the most important markets in the Middle Ages were the wool markets, such as the one in the French town of Calais. This market was called the 'staple'. All English wool sent abroad was sold there. There were other important cloth markets all over Europe, especially in Holland and Italy.

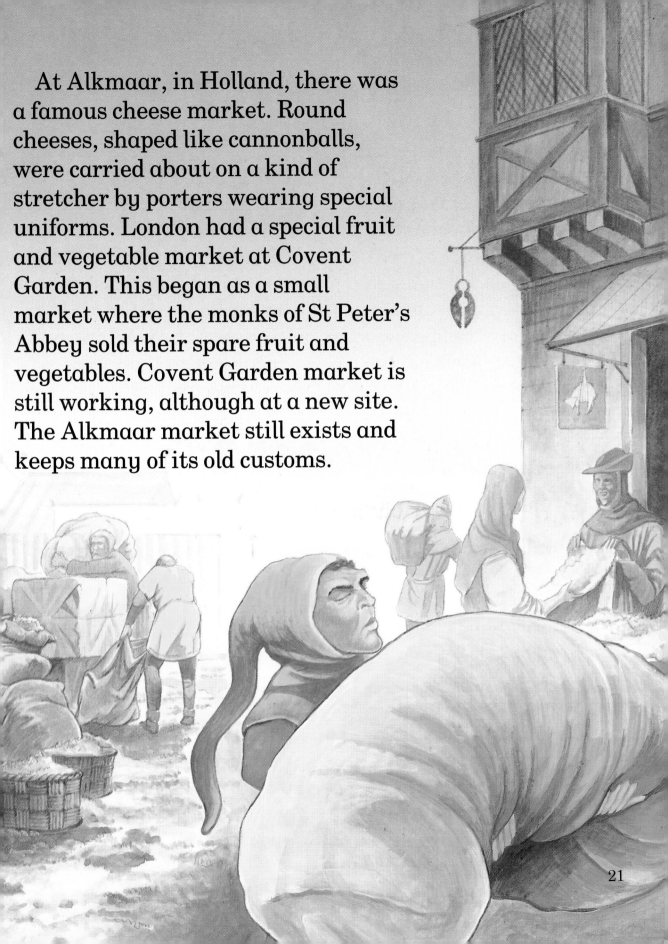

At Alkmaar, in Holland, there was a famous cheese market. Round cheeses, shaped like cannonballs, were carried about on a kind of stretcher by porters wearing special uniforms. London had a special fruit and vegetable market at Covent Garden. This began as a small market where the monks of St Peter's Abbey sold their spare fruit and vegetables. Covent Garden market is still working, although at a new site. The Alkmaar market still exists and keeps many of its old customs.

GLOSSARY

Barter Swapping goods, not exchanging them for money.

Blacksmith Someone who makes things out of iron and other metals, for example axes, nails and weapons.

Council A group of people who decide how a town or city should be run.

Craftsman Someone who is very skilled at making a particular kind of object.

Jousting A sport in which horsemen try to knock each other off their horses with lances.

Juggler A skilful entertainer who throws and catches several balls, or other objects, so that some of them are always in the air.

Medieval To do with the Middle Ages.

Merchant Someone who makes a living by buying and selling.

Middle Ages The period between about AD1000 and 1500.

Minstrel An entertainer who played a musical instrument and sang.

Monastery A place where monks spent their lives working for God.

Pedlar A person who travelled about selling small goods.

Pillory A wooden frame with holes for heads and hands, where people were locked up as a punishment.

Stocks A wooden frame with holes for the feet, where people were locked as punishment.

Toll A charge which has to be paid to use a market, road or bridge.

Yardstick A stick, about 1 metre in length, used to measure cloth.

BOOKS TO READ

Markets by Cherry Gilchrist (Cambridge University Press, 1983).

Medieval Times edited by Molly Lodge (Hodder & Stoughton, 1985).

Middle Ages by Barry Steel and Anne Steel (Wayland, 1986).

Shopping in History by Sheila Robertson (Wayland, 1984).

Picture acknowledgements

The publishers would like to thank the following for providing the photographs in this book: Ancient Art and Architecture collection 8 (top), 11 (top), 17 (bottom); Michael Holford 6 (top), 11 (bottom); Macdonald/Aldus Archive 13 (top); Peter Newark's Historical Pictures 17 (top); Ronald Sheridan 6 (bottom), 8 (bottom).

INDEX